Brush Lettering

— the ultimate guide —

Peggy Dean
The Pigeon Letters

The Ultimate Brush Lettering Guide: A Complete Step-by-Step Creative Workbook to Jump Start Modern Calligraphy Skills

ISBN 978-0-9985585-0-9

Second edition 2017

10 9 8 7 6 5 4 3 2

Dedicated to
Laura
♡
thank you
for
believing in my
journey
before I even
knew I had one.

contents

I like to think of modern brush lettering as a new age twist on ornate calligraphy mixed with whimsical hand lettering. It's an artistic, structured tribute to swoon-worthy handwriting.

This book will guide you through your very own brush lettering journey and before you know it, you'll be creating beautiful designs with a developed style unique only to you.

Every
adventure
requires
a first
step

– cheshire cat

what to Expect

In the following comprehensive lessons, you will discover tips and tricks for basic letter forms, connective spacing while creating words, and the buildup of more elaborate, flourished designs.

With focus on structure and design, you'll be prepared to take on a variety of stylistic approaches. This book breaks down the methods used to correctly apply brush strokes. Aside from learning lettering, beginning with brush pens is a learning curve itself. You will get familiar with how to properly use brush tips, as its varying thickness from applied pressure can make or break your work.

You will also learn the highly desired techniques such as adding bounce to your lettering, incorporating color and patterns, and integrating other mediums, along with additional effects to your letters. You will also be taken through step-by-step instructions in a variety of projects to ignite inspiration and creativity.

Practice makes progress

THE BEAUTY BEHIND HAND LETTERING IS IN THE IMPERFECTIONS. LEARNING HOW TO MASTER FLAWS AND CHANNEL THEM, CREATING CHARACTER, IS WHAT MAKES YOUR BRAND UNIQUE TO YOU. BREAKING DOWN THESE ELEMENTS WILL GIVE YOU THAT FOUNDATION THAT YOU CAN CONFIDENTALLY BUILD YOUR CRAFT UPON.

OH, AND ONE MORE THING — DON'T BE AFRAID TO FAIL.

If you cannot fail, you cannot learn

eric ries

A Note of Inspiration

Inspiration pops up in basic, every day moments. It's up to us to pay attention. It's inccredibly easy to get caught up in comparison, fear, repetition, discouragement... the list goes on.

Making the first move is easily the most difficult. There are so many things to overthink—

Here are a few Q & As:

pick up the pen

that's probably true, but not the way you will.

learning is the fun part

- WHERE DO I START?
- SOMEBODY MAY HAVE ALREADY DONE IT.
- SOMEBODY MAY HAVE ALREADY DONE IT ~BETTER~ *differently*
- I DON'T KNOW HOW.
- THAT ONE TIME I TRIED, IT WAS A DISASTER.
- AM I TALENTED ENOUGH? — *two words: acquired skills*
- I DON'T HAVE TIME.
- I CAN'T AFFORD IT.
- I DON'T HAVE ANY EXPERIENCE.

Practice makes progress

15 minutes a day.

Even better! you have the opportunity to learn the ~RIGHT~ way

check my tools and materials section for budget friendly options

So where do you start?

learn

If you're reading this book, you're already off to a great start. You will have the knowledge of important fundamentals, which allow an easier time picking up new techniques to advance you into other levels of your potential.

Be sure to source knowledge from many avenues, as you may discover an even more productive learning style. Some excellent resource channels include books, blogs, workshops, online classes, videos, social media, and more. View my resources section toward the end of this book for a plethora of direct suggestions, including The Pigeon Letters' complete list (that's me)!

network

Connect with others in the industry via online communication, local meet-ups, and social media. Just bouncing passion off of other creates can be a huge boost in motivation and has potential to sprout amazing ideas.

collaborate

Collaboration is a fun part of networking. This could include working together with another artist in a particular project or ideas on a grander scale. Working alongside others in the maker community is extremely beneficial. There's a small handful of us -vs- the population, and it's very rewarding to embrace

community over competion.

then

practice

practice

practice

practice

practice

practice

practice

practice

practice

Allow yourself to be a beginner. No one starts off being excellent.

Wendy Flynn

Here are just a few ways hand lettering can be incorporated:

Weddings

Font Design

logo design

Testimonials

Religious Art

Announcements

graphic Design

Invitations

Maps

Certificates

the Toolbox

Having the right tools and materials is essential to your success in your lettering journey. Your pens matter. Your paper matters. There are so many options out there, so I've created a comprehensive guide of some of my favorite go-to supplies.

$$$

A note: Purchasing your first lettering beginners' kit doesn't have to break the bank. Reference my budget friendly guide at the end of this section (and you might be surprised at how little you need to get started).

Brush Pens

BRUSH TIP SIZE	FLEXIBILITY SCALE	CONTROL LEVEL SCALE
small 1–10 large	low 1–10 high	low 1–10 high

A) Prismacolor Premier Marker
- SMALL BRUSH TIP - 4
- FLEXIBILITY - 9
- CONTROL - 5
- SMALL TO MEDIUM LETTERING

B) Tombow Fydendsuke Hard & Soft Tip
- SMALL BRUSH TIP - 3
- FLEXIBILITY - 3,4
- CONTROL - 7,8
- SMALL TO MEDIUM LETTERING

C) Pentel Fude Touch Sign Pen
- SMALL BRUSH TIP - 4
- FLEXIBILITY - 6
- CONTROL - 6
- SMALL TO MEDIUM LETTERING

D) Pentel Aquash
- SMALL, MEDIUM & BOLD - 5,8,10
- FLEXIBILITY - 10
- CONTROL - 5
- MEDIUM TO LARGE LETTERING

E) Tombow Dual Brush Pen
- LARGE BRUSH TIP - 9
- FLEXIBILITY - 5
- CONTROL - 7
- LARGE LETTERING

A   B   C   D   E

GREAT FOR BEGINNERS!

19

MONO PENS

A) *Micron*
Pigma Ink Pens

- FADE RESISTANT
- SEVERAL COLORS
- MANY SIZE OPTIONS
- PERMANENT
- DOESN'T BLEED

B) *papermate*
Flair

- POINT GUARD FELT TIP
- DOESN'T BLEED
- 26 COLORS

C) *Uni-Ball*
Gel Impact

- VISIBLE INK SUPPLY
- OPAQUE
- WRITES ON MOST SURFACES

D) *Zebra*
Sakura Gel

- FAST DRYING
- SMUDGE PROOF
- 14 VIBRANT COLORS
- MANY SIZES

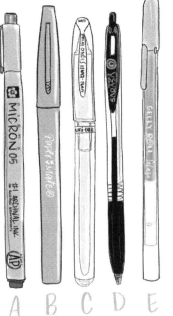

E) *Gelly Roll*
by Sakura

- FINE & MEDIUM POINT
- SEVERAL COLOR SETS/
  FINISHES (CLASSIC, STARDUST,
  METALLIC, GOLD SHADOW,
  SOUFFLE, MOONLIGHT, ETC.)

A   B   C   D   E

paper

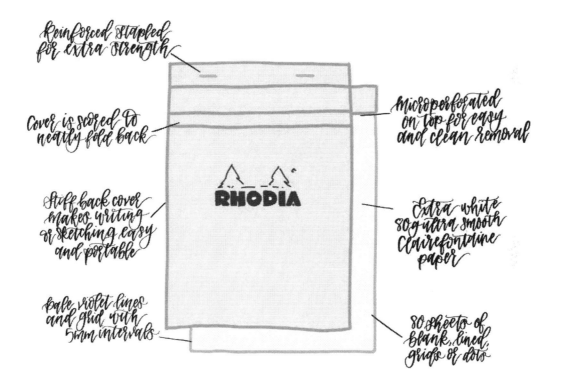

Reinforced stapled for extra strength

Cover is scored to neatly fold back

Stiff back cover makes writing or sketching easy and portable

Pale violet lines and grid with 5mm intervals

Microperforated on top for easy and clean removal

Extra white 80g ultra smooth Clairefontaine paper

80 sheets of blank, lined, grids or dots

RHODIA

A lot of folks don't realize that most paper can ruin brush pens. Copy/printer paper, for example, contains micro fibers that will shred the tips of brush pens which causes them to fray, rendering them useless. In a short amount of time, it will seem as though the ink has run out or the tips don't stay sharp, and this begins and ends with the care of the brush tips.

Rhodia pads are an excellent choice for most lettering practice and projects. Its silky surface is the perfect partner to a brush pen's glide. Additionally, any paper that specifies use with "markers" is usually a safe bet.

When using water brushes, it is recommended that paper made specifically for water media be used. This paper should be 140 lb/300 g at minimum, acid free, and textured.

ON A TIGHT BUDGET?
Just grab these!

TOMBOW FUDENOSUKE 2-PACK
HARD & SOFT TIP BRUSH PENS

RHODIA DOT PAD
(OR BLANK)

Anything's possible if you've got enough nerve.

J.K. Rowling

NOTE, DOUBLE NOTE AND TRIPLE NOTE:

Lettering IS NOT handwriting!

When lettering, you do not simply begin writing and then applying techniques. You are, instead, drawing. Calligraphic letters of all styles require a consistent base shape which creates uniformity across an alphabet. Even modern calligraphy's loose, whimsical style demands attention to structure.

Lettering IS NOT

- meant to be perfect
- a skill acquired overnight
- typography
- calligraphy — Huh?

practice make progress!

That's right. It's confusing and contradictory. Let's break it down.

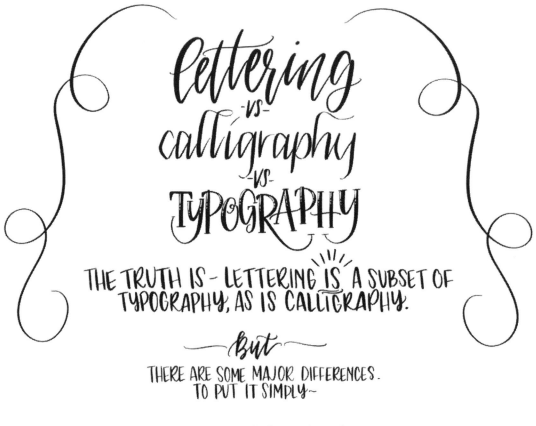

Lettering -vs- calligraphy -vs- TYPOGRAPHY

THE TRUTH IS - LETTERING IS A SUBSET OF TYPOGRAPHY, AS IS CALLIGRAPHY.

But

THERE ARE SOME MAJOR DIFFERENCES. TO PUT IT SIMPLY ~

Hand lettering is **the art of drawing letters.**

what is it?

Lettering should be viewed from the perspective of its overall design. It is focused on composition and is created as an art piece. It is a specific combination of letters that create a single piece.

Letters are drawn, not written.

How's it done?

Brush pens are primarily used to combine letters organically into a piece that is one-of-a-kind. Each letter takes on its own character, and the same letter will not display identically when drawn again. Letters are positioned to create a unique image which can be considered an illustration. This can also be done with in a monoline style applied to create a variety of designs.

What's it used for?

Piece are created to showcase one design only. If its letters were taken part from its puzzle and placed elsewhere, they wouldn't fit into a new puzzle. This makes lettering a custom illustrative design every single time.

Lettering creates READABLE art that comes to LIFE, displaying a quirky, whimsical nature.

Peggy Dean

Calligraphy is **the art of writing letters**.

What is it?

Calligraphy is a single pass with a pen to write letters. It is a personalized, lovely writing form often used to compose letters, and is based on penmanship. It is an emotional form of writing, typically very meaningful to its recipients. Writing letters uses the same lettering style throughout, using muscle memory as you would your own handwriting.

How's it done?

Calligraphy is formed using a pointed pen using a nib that dips into ink or with a fountain pen in which the ink flows to the nib as it's used. Its stroke is gone over only once with a single pass (whereas lettering uses multiple passes), connecting words and sentences to create ornamental memorabilia.

What's it used for?

Beautiful penmanship is often found in personal letters, wedding stationery, and more.

CALLIGRAPHY'S LITERAL MEANING IS *beautiful writing*.

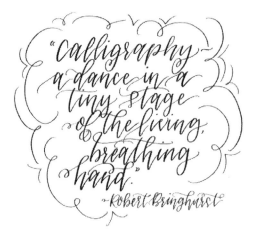

"Calligraphy —
a dance in a
tiny stage
of the living,
breathing
hand."
~Robert Bringhurst

Typography is **the study of letters applied to typefaces** and how letter forms interact on a surface.

What is it?

It's a collection of physical characters that are designed and created for reuse. Typography's similarity to hand lettering lies in displaying letter forms on a surface to create a composition. However, it is digitally based and created by typeface designers and commonly used by graphic designers. An easy way to distinguish typography is to recognize it as a font which is a collection of prefabricated letters.

How's it done?

Typeface designers put a lot of work into creating fonts. They formulate letters that work together in endless combinations, which takes a high level of skill and a lot of devoted time. There are several different software programs that can be used such as Adobe Illustrator. To design, letter forms are built up bit-by-bit, perfecting their shape and style.

What's it used for?

Typography is used everywhere: books, websites, brochures, signs, logos, and more, more, more...

BEFORE WE DIVE INTO THE EXPLORATIVE JOURNEY OF LETTERING, I STRONGLY ENCOURAGE YOU TO MAKE PHOTOCOPIES OF YOUR FAVORITE PRACTICE SHEETS FROM THE FOLLOWING PAGES. ALTHOUGH THERE ARE SPACES FOR PRACTICE THROUGHOUT THIS BOOK, IT WILL BE HELPFUL TO HAVE EXTRAS ON HAND!

33

34

THE Anatomy OF lettering

downstroke

head   shoulder

tail

hairline   stem

exit stroke

upstroke

flourish

lead-in stroke

swash
EXAGGERATED SERIF

B B B

crossbar
HORIZONTAL STROKE

A H

ligature
TWO OR MORE LETTERS COMBINED
TO MAKE A SINGLE CHARACTER

coffee

flourish
A DECORATIVE, ORNAMENTAL STROKE
(SWASHES ARE IN THIS CATEGORY)

- LIGATURES

the adventure

- MOOD

whimsical
sweet
romantic
bubbly

- BOUNCE

dream

REGULAR

dream

BOUNCE

Learn the rules like a pro so you can break them like an artist

— PABLO PICASSO —

guidelines
— what are all those lines? —

ASCENDER
CAP HEIGHT
X-HEIGHT *Whimsy*
BASELINE
DESCENDER

ASCENDER
PART OF LOWERCASE LETTERS THAT
MAY RISE ABOVE THE CAP HEIGHT

CAP HEIGHT
THE HEIGHT OF A CAPITAL LETTER

X-HEIGHT
THE DISTANCE BETWEEN THE BASELINE
AND THE MEAN LINE OF LOWERCASE LETTERS

BASELINE
THE AREA IN WHICH THE TEXT "SITS"

DESCENDER
THE PORTION OF LETTERS THAT DIP
BELOW THE BASELINE

You'll find that traditional calligraphy has a hard focus on the structure and shape of letters, while modern lettering has a strong emphasis on ll the unique ways to stretch traditional rules.

TRADITIONAL
CALLIGRAPHY — *Whimsy*

MODERN
CALLIGRAPHY — *Whimsy*

Modern lettering allows for a softer, rounder, looser letter form. It can be intentionally irregular, which largely contributes to its charm.

letter formation

:: USE FOUR CORNERS
:: AS A GUIDE

CREATE BASE
SHAPE

abcd   *abcd*

EXAMPLE #1 UTILIZES ALL TOUCH POINTS
EXAMPLE #2 UTILIZES ONLY THREE:

KEEP PARALLEL LINES *a/m* AXIS

KEEP CONSISTENT HEIGHT AND SPACE

do this → b d g h j k l q

not this → b d g h j k l q

NOTE: IT'S FINE IF YOU PREFER MORE OR LESS HEIGHT/SPACE
AS LONG AS ALL YOUR LETTERS REMAIN IN UNIFORM
(the G, K, & L would be a great style grouping)

Practice utilizing touch points

USE A REGULAR
BALLPOINT PEN
TO FORM YOUR
LETTER SHAPES

letter forms

Learn how to build letters before building words.
Try lifting your [regular] pen after your first strokes for more control.

example

a a

b b

c c

d d

e e

f f

g g

h h

i i

j j

letter forms

Notice the base shape of each letter as you practice building them.
Are the shapes uniform?

letter forms

Practicing a steady pattern will give you the tools to branch into your own style.

u u

v v

w w

x x

y y

z z

KEEP GOING!
CONTINUE THE LETTERS THAT YOU FIND MORE CHALLENGING.

let's connect!

There are several factors to consider when determining how you will connect your letters. Understanding the relationships between letters will allow you to break the rules and get creative.

• LENGTH OF LEAD-IN/EXIT STROKES

dandelion

dandelion

NARROW

dandelion

LONG

• DIRECTION OF LEAD-IN/EXIT STROKES

labrador

SOFT CURVE UPWARD

labrador

HARD CURVE UP AND "OVER"

Rules for making words

Connections can be tricky when too much thought is put into them. Remember the following rules and you'll find this process to be much easier.

RULE #1-

Stop your exit stroke before beginning the next letter. Lift your pen off the paper for each break. Basically, treat each letter as a stand-alone letter.

THIS WILL COME IN HANDY WHEN YOU BEGIN INCORPORATING FLOURISHES!

rainbow

For example, here are all the places I stopped, lifted my pen, then continued the next letter.

RULE #2 -

Don't worry about your connecting lines matching up perfectly.

Notice where my "n" connects to my "b" in both examples. I didn't worry about where the lead-in for my "b" would connect. Rather, I treated it as its own beginning.

Here is the same rule with a flourish incorporated.

rainbow

RULE #3 -

Be sure that your connecting strokes are consistent in length. This is why:

Even with a solid base shape, if spacing is inconsistent, the word can turn out a bit sloppy.

SHORT · LONG   DON'T DO THIS!

waterfall

(DO THIS INSTEAD)

CONSISTENT SHORTER SPACING

(OR THIS)

waterfall

CONSISTENT LONGER SPACING

PRACTICE
CREATING WORDS

find your style
tip
TRY lettering
the same word
- with short spacing
- with long spacing

WELL NOW THAT WE'VE COME THIS FAR, HOW ABOUT A PROPER INTRODUCTION?

Write your name using your new letter formations.

DON'T FEEL RESTRICTED. USE THE DOT GRID AS A GUIDE, BUT NOT TO STAY INSIDE THE BOXES.

HELLO
my name is

HOW ABOUT SOME MORE ABOUT you!

OCCUPATION:

HOBBIES:

faux calligraphy

Once you feel comfortable with your letters, you can begin to add weight to them. We're not quite ready for the brush pen though, so don't jump in just yet! We will begin adding weight using a nifty technique called **faux calligraphy**.

It's easy! Here's how you do it.

When you write a letter, pay attention to your upstrokes and downstrokes.

abcd

Instructions:

Draw a line very close to the downstrokes of your letters, connecting the lines at the beginning and end of the weight line.

abcdefg
hijklm
nopqrs
tuvwxyz

get the look

After familiarizing yourself with weight line placement, all you need to do is fill in the white space. You can do this by coloring in the empty space which imitate the appearance of a brush pen.

EXAMPLE

STEP ONE:
USE CONSISTENT BASE SHAPES TO LETTER A WORD

STEP TWO:
ADD WEIGHT LINE TO DOWNSTROKES

STEP THREE:
COLOR IN WHITE SPACE

strawberry

FOLLOW THE PROMPTS TO PRACTICE
adding weight

tip
keep the same
distance between
each letter and
its weight
line

favorite color

favorite flower

hometown

best friend

favorite animal

role model

Add some spunk!

I encourage you to use your creativity and draw a pattern inside the empty space. Fill this space with a color other than black. Try using pink, blue or yellow!

tip
try using
alternating
colors in letters
and/or words

PATTERN PLAY
HOW MANY CAN YOU COME UP WITH?

I'm still learning.

—michelangelo, age 87

Brush Lettering 101

YOU'VE GOTTEN PRETTY COMFORTABLE WITH YOUR BASE SHAPES? SWELL!

FEEL GOOD ABOUT WHERE TO ADD WEIGHT TO YOUR LETTERS? SUPER!

ARE YOU READY FOR THE brush pen? let's go!

Keeping all previous lessons in mind, add this rule:

Press firmly on your downstrokes.
This causes the brush to flatten and create a thicker downstroke (aka adds weight).

AND

Release pressure on your upstrokes.
This will make the brush return to its pointed tip.

Basic Strokes

Full Pressure

| | | | | |

The thick stroke that begins and ends with a thick, full-bellied motion

Entry Stroke

The hairline stroke leading into the beginning of a letter

Underturn

U U U U U

The scooping U-shaped stroke that begins with a thick downstroke and curves upward in a scooping motion into a thin, hairline upstroke

Overturn

The arched upside-down U-shaped stroke that begins with a thin upstroke and curves over into a thick downstroke.

Compound Curve

Combines the under turn and overturn strokes to create a seamless wavy stroke

Oval

Combines the under turn stroke and overturn stroke creating an enclosed rounded shape

Ascending Stem Loop

ℓ ℓ ℓ ℓ ℓ

The stroke beginning in an upward, hairline curve, transitioning into a thick stroke downward

Descending Stem Loop

ʃ ʃ ʃ ʃ ʃ

The thick stroke moving downward, then curving upward into a thin line that meets the middle of the downstroke

It's crucial that you familiarize yourself with these basic strokes and continue returning to these practices along your lettering journey. Each brush pen is unique in its flexibility and size, so these basics will come in handy while breaking in those new tools.

TAKE A CLOSER LOOK AT DOWNSTROKES AND UPSTROKES

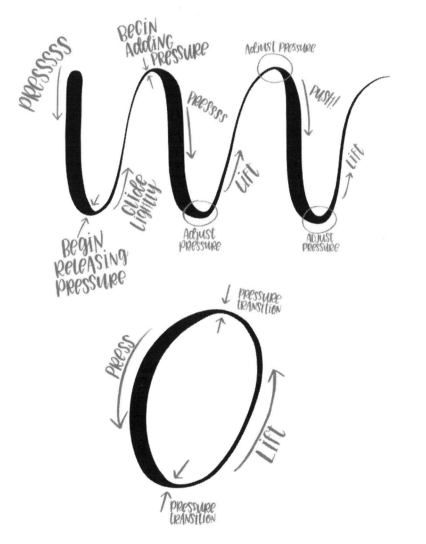

BASIC STROKES

DOWNSTROKES |||||| //////
UPSTROKES |||||| //////

|||||||

//////

UNDERTURN U U U U U U
OVERTURN ∩∩∩∩∩∩

U U U U U

∩∩∩∩∩∩∩

BASIC STROKES

ENTRY STROKE /////

FULL PRESSURE |||||||||

COMPOUND CURVE

BASIC STROKES

OVAL O O O O O O

O O O O *O* *O* *O*

ASCENDER LOOP STEM ℓ ℓ ℓ ℓ ℓ ℓ
DESCENDER LOOP STEM ∫ ∫ ∫ ∫ ∫ ∫

ℓ ℓ ℓ ℓ *ℓ* *ℓ* *ℓ* *ℓ*

∫ ∫ ∫ ∫ *∫* *∫* *∫* *∫*

Now we'll use these brush strokes in our letters.

You will find some of these brush stokes in the following:

∩ OVERTURN *a b c d e g h m n p q*

∪ UNDERTURN *e g q s u w y*

○ OVAL *a b d g k o p q*

⟍⟋ COMPOUND CURVE *M* OFTEN FOUND COMBINED WHEN ENTRY STROKES

∫ ASCENDER STEM LOOP *b d f h k l*

∫ DESCENDER STEM LOOP *f g j q y z*

try it out!

UNDERSTROKE

OVAL

UNDERSTROKE

DESCENDER STEM LOOP

Left-Handed?

You can just as successfully learn to master lettering as your right-handed neighbor.

THE STRUGGLE (IS REAL)

The biggest road block for both "lefties" and "righties" always comes down to mental barriers. You will be the only one holding you back. If this block stemmed from the feeling of failure, perhaps due to a messy attempt complete with an ink-stained hand and smudged up paper, hold onto this thought:

First
Attempt
In
Learning

Mental barriers can exist without having tried yet because of fear of failure. Well guess what -

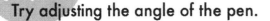

Everybody starts somewhere.

Here are a couple tips for left-handed aspiring letterers.

Try adjusting the angle of the pen.

Left-handed writers are both underwriters (keeping the wrist straight and holding the pen above) and also overwriters (curling the wrist and holding the pen underneath).

If you're an overwriter, you may be familiar with smudging your work as your hand follows.

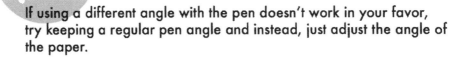

If using a different angle with the pen doesn't work in your favor, try keeping a regular pen angle and instead, just adjust the angle of the paper.

what are you trying to say?

Do you ever see a piece that makes you feel a particular way? Perhaps a chalkboard advertising fresh navel oranges, making you sense its citrus texture? Or a stunning, delicate wedding invitation invoking the fragile feeling of precious love? How about an eye-catching sleek, modern business card that gives you confidence that the company or individual is the real deal?

These mood-invoking designs are largely due to their stylistic choices of their lettering.

EXAMPLES:

whimsy *Bubbly*
PLAYFUL *Airy*

The following pages present 10 different ways to create each uppercase letter, 10 ways for each lowercase letter, and 10 ways to create numbers.

Alphabet Style

uppercase & lowercase

10 WAYS   10 WAYS

68

Alphabet Style
uppercase & lowercase
≈10 WAYS≈ ≈10 WAYS≈

Alphabet Style

uppercase & lowercase

10 WAYS   10 WAYS

Alphabet Style

Uppercase & Lowercase

Alphabet Style

10 WAYS · **10 WAYS**

Alphabet Style

Uppercase & Lowercase

10 WAYS   10 WAYS

Alphabet Style

Uppercase & Lowercase
~10 Ways~ ~10 Ways~

Alphabet Style

uppercase & lowercase

Alphabet Style

uppercase & lowercase

10 WAYS   10 WAYS

Alphabet Style

Uppercase & Lowercase

=10 WAYS=   =10 WAYS=

Intro to bounce

When a letter's exit stroke is naturally directed downward, you can dip below the descender line.

thank you

DIP
BASELINE
DIP
BASELINE
BASELINE
DIP

MEET BACK AT THE BASELINE TO MAINTAIN BALANCE.

When the exit stroke naturally drags upward, you can reach above the ascender line.

hello

REACH
REACH
REACH
REACH
BASELINE

Practice your bounce

tip
return to baseline every few letters

CHOOSE AN ANIMAL.
LETTER IT A FEW DIFFERENT WAYS
USING BOUNCE LETTERING.

CROSS BARS

A
A
A

H
H
H

SERIFS

A
D
R

V
D
C

Create
your own!

tip
Avoid crossing thick lines with other thick lines

practice creating ascenders AND descenders

Let's play Make Believe

Did you ever use made up words as a kid? Do you recall any crazy combinations of letters or sounds?

Well, you get to revisit that time and create new made-up word.

Time to Brainstorm

USE THIS BOX TO JOT DOWN YOUR WORD IDEAS.

Once you've chosen your favorite, display it proudly! Write it here.

You've got your word, but it needs a definition!

_____

YOUR WORD

DEFINITION ↘

CIRCLE ONE: NOUN Adjective VERB

Do you find that you feel differently reading
"sweet" in these different styles?

↓   ↓

sweet   *Sweet*

Depending on the style applied to a word's structure, it will naturally
translate to different moods, creating a unique feel to each variation.

Let's give your word some new vibes! Use the prompts to letter your freshly created word.

let's see it...

shallow
X-HEIGHT

deep
X-HEIGHT

bounce

slanted

bubbly

long

flourishes

There is so much variety to explore!

let's see it...

faux

wide

skinny

eyes closed

slow

fast

NON-dominant Hand

Creativity has the ability to blossom with hand lettering. Incorporate some **variety**!

There's a lot you can do with even more simple letters such as "c" and "o," which wouldn't seem like they'd have much variety, but surprise!

Try 10 different swashes. Circle your favorite.

Try some new exit strokes.

Try dropping beneath the descender a few times.

Try drawing a
different style for
each letter.

You got this.

Practice varying degrees of understrokes. Make some higher and others lower.

Numeric Style

:10 WAYS:

1 2 3 4 5 6 7 8 9 0

1 2 3 4 5 6 7 8 9 0

1 2 3 4 5 6 7 8 9 0

1 2 3 4 5 6 7 8 9 0

1 2 3 4 5 6 7 8 9 0

1 2 3 4 5 6 7 8 9 0

1 2 3 4 5 6 7 8 9 0

1 2 3 4 5 6 7 8 9 0

1 2 3 4 5 6 7 8 9 0

1 2 3 4 5 6 7 8 9 0

Practice Numbers

How many different styles can you think of for each number?

A flourish is an ornamental flowing curve used to embellish lettering designs.

Simple flourishes are a lovely addition to words and designs that don't necessarily need to stand out, but that could benefit from a softer polished appearance.

Elaborate flourishes transform a basic design by adding a high degree of elegance. The addition of fancy flourishes alone can complete a logo, a greeting card, an announcement, a menu, and more.

Where to add flourishes:
- at the beginning/end of a word
- at the top of an ascending stem
- at the bottom of a descending tail

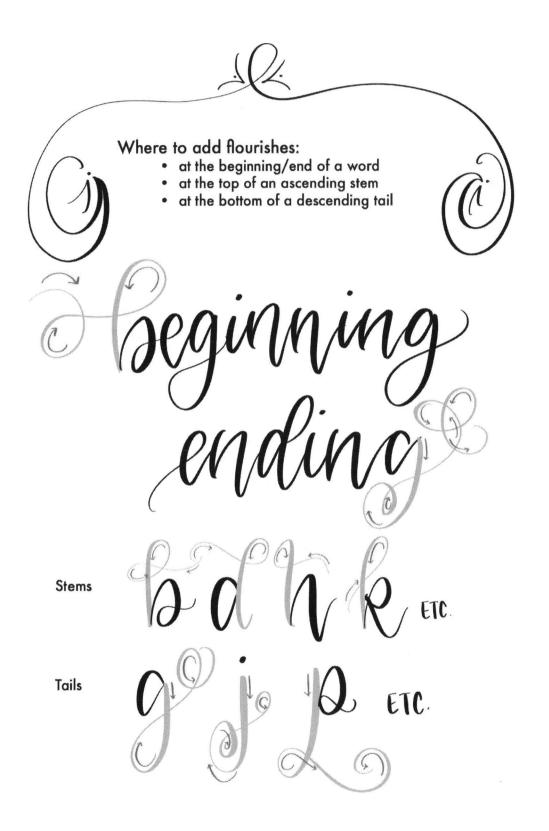

beginning

ending

Stems

b d h R ETC.

Tails

g j L ETC.

Look at the differences of a basic word after adding simple
flourishes and elaborate flourishes.

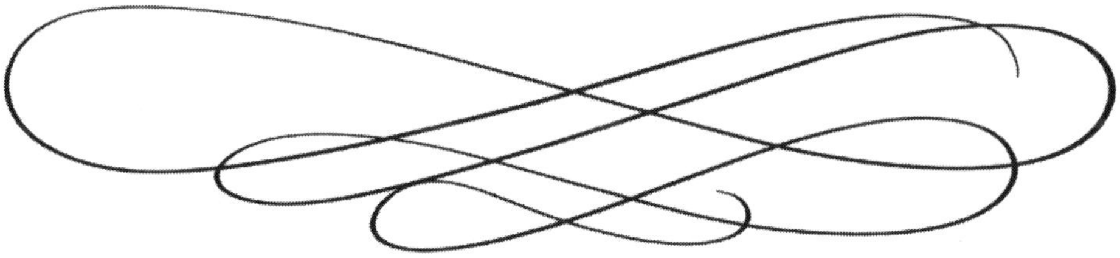

Basic bounce lettering

apple

Simple flourishes

apple

Elaborate flourishes

apple

Flourishes can also be used for clever ligatures.

in common words

the and

in names

Kate Sarah Anthony

in longer words

limitless

adventure

in occurances of repeating letters

lettering

scribble

STANDALONE FLOURISHES

Let's not forget about all the design possibilities awaiting when we incorporate flourishes that are not attached to letters. These add-ons are used with existing flourished words, as page dividers, as underlines, etc.

There are many styles of standalone flourishes to consider when setting the mood of your piece. Here are some examples to get you started.

SINGLE LINE   DOUBLE LINE

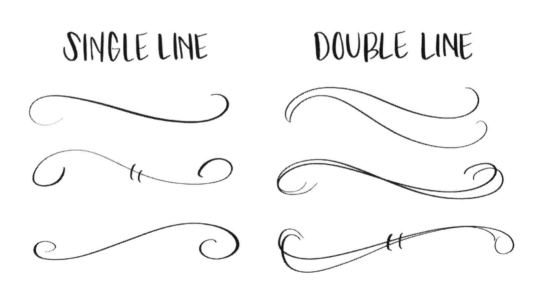

STANDALONE FLOURISHES

LOOPS

CURLS

STANDALONE FLOURISHES

BUILDABLE

Practice Decorative Flourishes

Composition

Using a pencil before using a brush pen can save you a lot of time and paper, as mistakes can be fixed. These examples feature several tips on how to best execute layouts.

3 WORDS - SAME SIZE

Place the middle word first.
This ensures the piece is centered.

Use the middle word as a guide for where your words above and below can reach and dip into the middle word's frame.

When you're happy with your composition, apply ink with your brush pen. If needed, erase any remaining pencil lines (but be sure the ink is completely dry first).

MULTIPLE WORDS WITH ATTENTION TO ONE.

Just as you placed your middle word as your guide, you will place your emphasized word first, making it larger than the other words will be.

Lettering the raining words in the same style is lovely and you can work inside the main word's frame as you did before.

That being said, mixing other lettering styles can be complimentary and add a more dynamic aesthetic.

STARS CAN'T *Shine* WITHOUT DARKNESS

MULTIPLE WORDS WITH FOCUS ON SEVERAL

First, lay our your main words that you want emphasized.

Add secondary words while using the main words as guides.

Add the remaining words to complete your composition.

If your dreams don't SCARE you, they're not big enough

Ellen Johnson Sirleaf

photograph your work

If you plan on taking photographs of your work, it's important to be aware of what's necessary to create high quality images, but also where you can cut corners.

Snap click

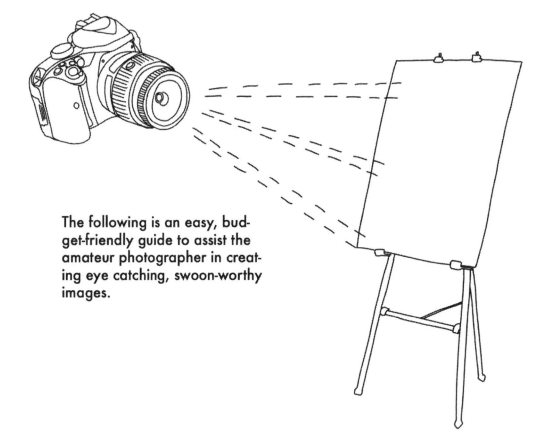

The following is an easy, budget-friendly guide to assist the amateur photographer in creating eye catching, swoon-worthy images.

Lighting

Lighting is, hands down, the most important aspect in producing images of professional quality. If you've got your light source covered, the rest falls into place.

Best — LARGE WINDOWS THAT LET IN NATURAL DAYLIGHT

good — STUDIO LIGHTING
- UMBRELLA
- SOFTBOX
- RINGLIGHT

okay — DAYLIGHT LIGHTBULBS

POOR — WARM LIGHTING

Camera

With technology's increasingly progressive design and functionality, a non-complex photo project no longer demands high tech equipment.

Best
DIGITAL SLR
+ PHOTO EDITING SOFTWARE

Good
· 2015+ SMARTPHONE
· DIGITAL CAMERA

POOR
· DISPOSABLE CAMERA
· WEBCAM

:tip
USING A FLEXIBLE ARM MOUNT WITH A SMARTPHONE WORKS GREAT TO CAPTURE VIDEO OF YOUR ART PROCESS

Composition

Creativity has an opportunity to really shine here. Consider the following key points when capturing your images.

What is the image going to be used for?

	Angle	Framing	Accents
ONLINE STORE	Head on	perimeter, at a distance	flowers, frame, colored/textured wall, trinkets
SOCIAL MEDIA	ANY! low & flush, tilted, above, side, head on	ANY! behind the scenes, with surrounding "props", close up, cropped	flowers, trinkets, colored/textured wall, nature supplies, twine, coffee, etc
BLOG	include multiple- to fully feature the piece "in different settings"	include multiple- to fully feature the piece "in different settings"	MINIMAL- colored/textured wall, supplies
PORTFOLIO	Head on	perimeter	NONE
PRINTS	Head on	perimeter	NONE

Enhance

Applying edits digitally allows for additional lighting adjustments. These are the main areas to focus on.

White Balance

TEMPERATURE

COOL

UNDERTONES:
BLUE
GREEN

NEUTRAL

THIS IS WHERE YOU
WANT TO BE.

WARM

UNDERTONES:
RED
ORANGE

Brightness

+ 20%

It's amazing what a difference a small bump in brightness can do to liven up an image.

HOW TO INSTAGRAM

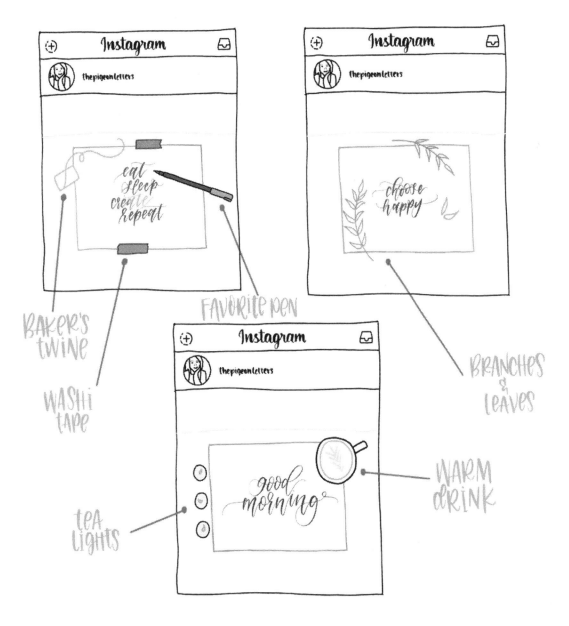

Instagram
thepigeonletters
eat
sleep
create
repeat

Instagram
thepigeonletters
choose
happy

Instagram
thepigeonletters
good
morning

BAKER'S TWINE

FAVORITE PEN

WASHI TAPE

BRANCHES & LEAVES

TEA LIGHTS

WARM DRINK

Common Hashtags to Keep on your Radar

#moderncalligraphy
#brushlettering
#lettering
#handlettering
#modernscript
#handwrittenfont
#handmadefont
#handdrawntype
#typographyinspired
#typematters
#pointedpen
#typespired
#calligrafriends
#artstagram
#qotd

#letteringchallenge
#thedailytype
#craftsposure
#goodtype
#letteringco
#calligraphymasters
#typeinspire
#dslettering
#typegang
#makersvillage
#creatorslane
#handletteredabcs
#calligrabasics
#learnlettering
#learncalligraphy

Now that you've equipped yourself with new knowledge and mad lettering skills, it's time to put it all to use in some projects!

Use the following pages to prompt the DIYer in your to start creating.

create a BUNTING

Step 1

tip
Be sure to cut your triangles wide enough to fit your letters

Select about two pieces of white card stock. You may need more depending on the length of your word/phrase.

Cut your card stock into long, triangular sections in the quantity as the number of letters that are in your word or phrase.

tip
Cutting a straight line after the triangles creates another batch

MATERIALS:
- CARDSTOCK
- Adhesive
- Scissors
- Hole Punch
- BRUSH PEN
- twine

Select the same amount of colored card stock as used from the white paper. Use the white pieces as a guide, and leaving a small border, cut triangles just a bit larger than the size of the first cuts.

tip
leave even more room on the top to allow for string

The background color will make the letters really **pop**!

Adhere the two pieces of card stock. Then, use a hole punch to create the space that the twine will be threaded through.

— STEP 4 —

Pull out enough twin so there is slack at the ends, and cut!

String the twine through, starting behind, then through again from the front toward the back.

— Step 6 —

AND ⇒VOILA!⇐ You can now grab a couple of thumb-tacks and hang your darling bunting!

Create Watercolor Place Cards

MATERIALS:
- Scissors
- Brush Pen
- Thick Watercolor or Mixed Media Paper
- Watercolors
- Small Paint Brush

— Step 1 —

Determine what size you'd like the face of your place cards. Double that size (this will allow for the fold so they stand up), and cut out the number of place cards you'll be using. A paper cutter can also be used.

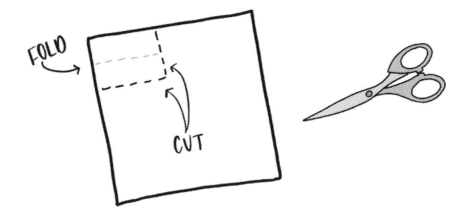

FOLD

CUT

— Step 2 —

Crease the middle to create a fold, then open and lay flat. You'll now be able to visually separate the front from the back, with the front below the crease.

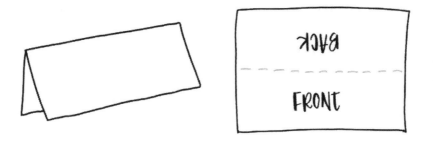

— Step 3 —

Lay a watercolor wash over the front area. This is where stylistic choices come into play. You can lay watercolor edge-to-edge or apply the wash to only a concentrated area.

Add an additional color or two for more vibrancy and dimension.

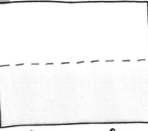

edge-to-edge

concentrated

— Step 4 —

After the watercolor dries, hand letter the names for your place cards directly on top of the dried paint.

lucy

— STEP 5 —

Refold, and you're ready to set up your place cards on a table.

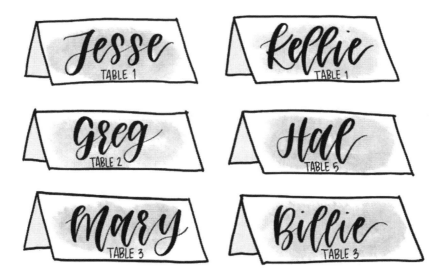

Silhouette Word Collage

STEP 1

Find an image with a clear outline.

STEP 2

Draw or trace only the outline of your image with **pencil**.

STEP 3

Hug the outline with words to preserve its shape.

USE A SILHOUETTE TO FRAME YOUR SUBJECT.

IDEAS OF WHAT TO INCLUDE:

PHYSICAL CHARACTERISTICS
PURPOSE IT SERVES
ROLES YOU MIGHT SEE IT IN
ALIASES/SYNONYMS/NICKNAMES

QUOTES/SONG LYRICS
WHERE IT'S COMMONLY FOUND
HOW IT MAKES YOU FEEL
ASSOCIATED THINGS

what if I fall?

Oh but darling, what if you fly

Emboss all the things!

Embossing is a fun finish to any project. You can add texture, shine, and sparkle to both simple and elaborate designs.

MATERIALS OVERVIEW

EMBOSSING POWDER
- glittery
- opaque
- metallic

HEAT TOOL
CONCENTRATED HIGH HEAT

EMBOSSING PENS
SPECIAL INK TO HOLD MOISTURE

There are a number of embossing tools to explore, and I encourage playing around with what is intriguing. Different effects can be made with different powder finishes. Project moods can be better interpreted by the color palette. Unlikely materials can be transformed by the unexpected embossed embellishments.

Sparkle Luster Glimmer Beam Shine Twinkle Dazzle Glisten Shimmer

Combinations can be challenged by exciting, new ideas.
For example

- black on black
- white on white
- clear only for texture effect and watercolor resistance
- orange on pink, red on blue, yellow on green, etc.

There are a variety of materials that can be embossed such as

- vellum
- envelopes
- notebooks
- terracotta
- ceramic
- wood
- glass
- and more

Although there are a lot of options, let's start easy with paper as a base.

Embossing pens have really opened the door for opportunity in design. Embossing pens can be found with brush tips, hard felt tips and even glue roller tips.

Step 1

Letter/draw the word(s)/design you will be embossing. You may want to first use a pencil to create your layout to eliminate unbalanced composition.

Sketch

Ink

tip:
DON'T INK THE
ENTIRE DESIGN IF ITS
LARGER/MORE
INTRICATE YOU DON'T
WANT TO RISK IT
DRYING OUT

Step 2

Lay embossing powder over the entire design, ensuring no areas are left exposed.

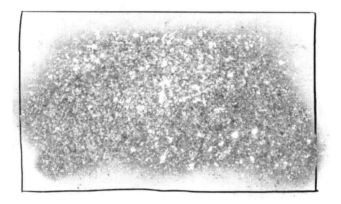

After the design has been covered, lift the paper and pour the powder off.

tip some powder will stick use a coarse dry paintbrush to sweep it away

The powder will remain only on the areas that the embossing pen was used.

Step 3

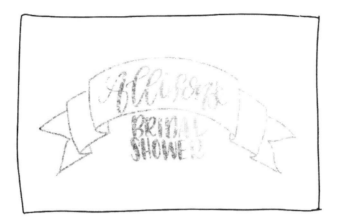

Holding the heat tool about 1.5 inches away from your piece, you will see the powder curing. This will be obvious because you will notice changes in color, shine, sparkle and texture. As you see the first part lift, "chase" the embossing by holding the heat tool at an angle and moving it across the design as it lifts as you go.

Once all of the powder has been cured, you are finished! It's that quick and easy.

Common Embossing Uh Ohs and Fixes

PAPER CURLING OR WARPING:

Turn the paper over and heat the backside. Depending on the thickness of the cardstock, this may need to be done several times.

PREVENT BURNING THE POWDER AND PAPER:

Move the tool as soon as you see the powder cure. Maintain a distance of about 1.5 inches between the paper and heat tool.

ALL DONE, BUT SOME AREAS AREN'T AS EMBOSSED:

This can occur if the ink wasn't wet enough when the powder was applied.
— FEAR NOT —
This is an easy fix! Just repeat each step over the areas that need it.

DON'T WASTE POWDER:

Use a scrap paper to catch the powder knocked loose from your design before it's cured. Pull the paper ends toward the middle and create a light crease/funnel, then pour the powder back into its container.

tip
going over a design 2-3 times will make it extra raised
pretty cool

PIECES OF MESSY EMBOSSING:

Loose powder will try to stick on your project like crumbs - where you don't want it! Here are some preventative tricks:
· Turn paper over and lightly tap or flick the backside
· Use a course, dry paintbrush and a light sweeping motion to dust off the loose powder

Envelopes get fancy

Envelope design can be so much fun. Use these examples for some inspiration.

mr & mrs Blanchard
123 Main Street
City, State
1 2 3 4 5

example 1
SIMPLE LETTERING WITH A LONG, EDGE-TO-EDGE NAME LINE

Annabelle James
123 MAIN ST.
CITY, STATE
1 2 3 4 5

example 2 ARCHED NAME

tip
use a pencil
to create an
arched
guideline

Natalie Baker
123 main st.
city, state 12345

example 3 BANNER

Bill Jones
123 Main St.
City, State

1 2 3 4 5

example 4 HEIGHT VARIATION

please deliver to...

Gayle Reuben

123 Main Street
City, State 12345

example 5 DELIVERY INSTRUCTION

Create a
botanical
alphabet
using
faux calligraphy

Let's get you familiar with some very easy, interchangeable floral doodles.

Step 1   Step 2   Step 3   ⸗DONE⸗

Step 1   Step 2   Step 3   ⸗DONE⸗

Step 1   Step 2   Step 3   ⸗DONE⸗

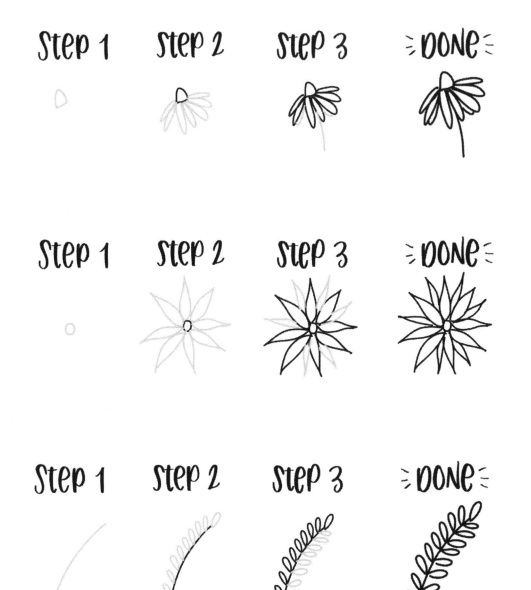

150

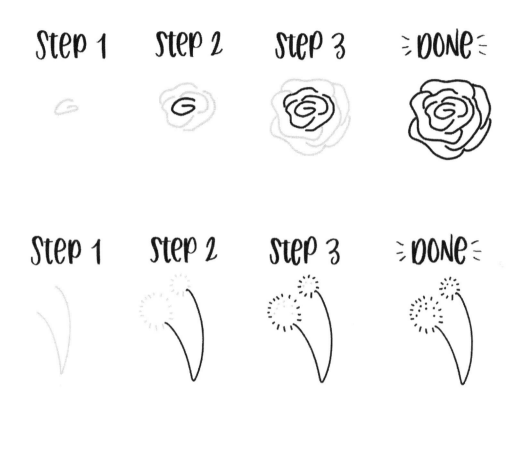

Step 1   Step 2   Step 3   ≥DONE≤

Step 1   Step 2   Step 3   ≥DONE≤

Step 1   Step 2   Step 3   ≥DONE≤

Step 1

Use a pencil to create your letters.

a b c

Step 2

Add flowers along one of the edges or in one isolated area in your letter's frame.

a b c

step 3

Use ink over the pencil lines, but be careful not to go over the floral lines.

step 4

Apply weight lines on the down strokes, as covered in the faux calligraphy segment. Again, don't draw through your flowers!

Step 5

Erase your pencil lines.

All done! You can keep your design as-is, or you can add patterns and/or color to the white space inside the weight lines.

Banner Design

Banners make for the perfect illustrated touch when adding them to your lettering pieces. They create statements and can be used in a number of ways including envelope addressing, logos, slogans, labels, greeting cards, and so much more. Banner designs vary from simple, basic styles to more ornate, flowing flags.

The following pages are some basic, step-by-step banners to get your started.

1.

2.

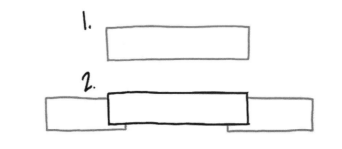

3.

4.

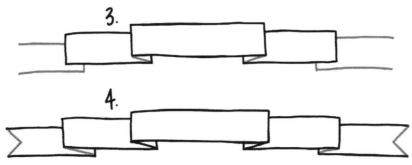

choose happy

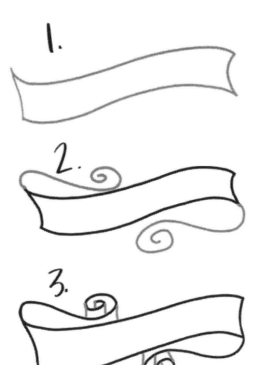

1.

2.

3.

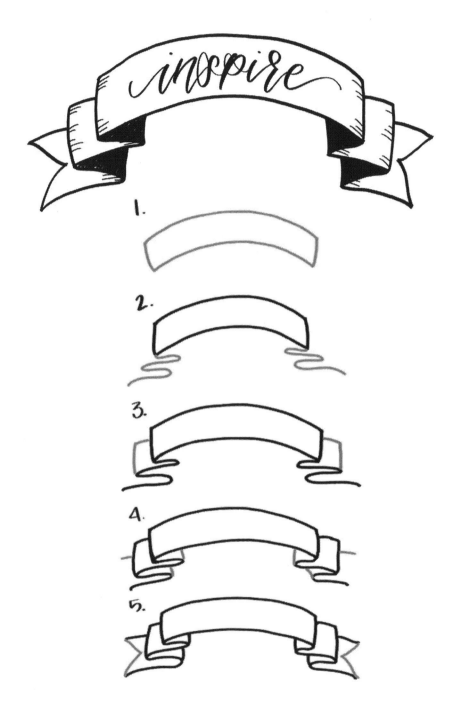

1.

2.

3.

4.

5.

1.

2.

3.

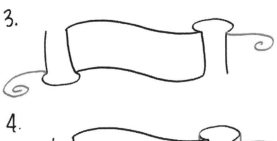

4.

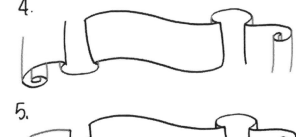

5.

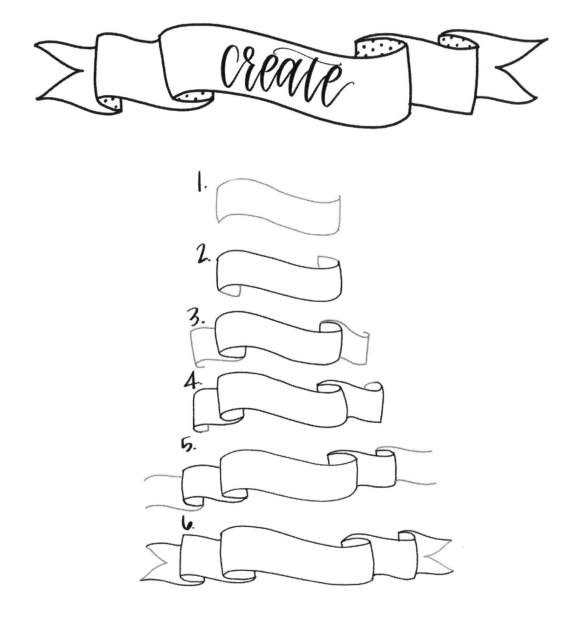

now go letter some pretties

lettering
Resources

learn
SKILLSHARE

ONLINE WATCH-AT-YOUR LEISURE COURSES
(MY CLASSES CHANNEL)
skillshare.com/r/thepigeonletters

NOTEWORTHY BLOGS

thepigeonletters   WWW.THEPIGEONLETTERS.COM

tombow   WWW.BLOG.TOMBOWUSA.COM

the inky hand   WWW.THEINKYHAND.COM
↳ lefties!

supplies
SEE TOOLS AND MATERIALS

shop
WWW.THEPIGEONLETTERS.ETSY.COM

▶ YOUTUBE.COM/C/THEPIGEONLETTERS

📷 @THEPIGEONLETTERS

About Peggy

hello

PACIFIC NORTHWEST GROWN
est. 1986

These are a few of my favorite things

SLIPPERS
MERMAIDS
SODA WATER
NINTENDO
CANDLES
BUBBLES
SWEATERS
TRAVEL

BOHEMIAN DECOR
WILD FLOWERS
EVERY SINGLE ANIMAL
PLAYDOH
PRECIOUS STONES
CHOCOLATE PUDDING
HOUSEPLANTS

I'M these →

hand letterer
illustrator
painter
instructor
platform Artist
DIYer

PUBLISHED HERE

Style Me Pretty
White Mag
Hochzeitswahn
Smitten Magazine
Oregon Bride Magazine

DISCOVER ADDITIONAL TIPS, DIY PROJECTS, ONLINE WATCH-AT-YOUR-LEISURE CLASSES, ART FOR PURCHASE, AND A PLETHORA OF MORE PRACTICE SHEETS BY VISITING

the blog

www.THEPIGEONLETTERS.com

index